THE DNA OF A MAN

TACTICAL GUIDE

ACTIVATE YOUR MASCULINE IDENTITY
REIGNITE YOUR DRIVE
AND WALK IN KINGDOM POWER

MATT HALLOCK ›

Copyright © 2025 Matt Hallock

www.manwarriorking.com

All rights reserved. This book or any part thereof may not be reproduced or transmitted in any form, including information storage and retrieval systems, without permission in writing from the publisher, except for the use of brief quotations in a book review.

For permission, visit www.manwarrior.com.

Unless otherwise indicated, all Scripture quotations are from The ESV® Bible (The Holy Bible, English Standard Version®), copyright © 2001 by Crossway. Used by permission. All rights reserved. Scripture quotations marked TPT are from The Passion Translation®. Copyright © 2017, 2018 by Passion & Fire Ministries, Inc. Used by permission. All rights reserved. ThePassionTranslation.com. Scripture quotations marked (NIV) are taken from the Holy Bible, New International Version®, NIV®. Copyright © 1973, 1978, 1984, 2011 by Biblica, Inc.™ Used by permission of Zondervan. All rights reserved worldwide. www.zondervan.com The "NIV" and "New International Version" are trademarks registered in the United States Patent and Trademark Office by Biblica, Inc.™ Scripture quotations marked NLT are taken from the Holy Bible, New Living Translation, copyright © 1996, 2004, 2015 by Tyndale House Foundation. Used by permission of Tyndale House Publishers, Inc., Carol Stream, Illinois 60188. All rights reserved. Scripture quotations marked NKJV are taken from the New King James Version®. Copyright © 1982 by Thomas Nelson. Used by permission. All rights reserved. Scripture quotations marked AMPC are taken from the Amplified® Bible (AMPC), Copyright © 1954, 1958, 1962, 1964, 1965, 1987 by The Lockman Foundation. Used by permission. www.Lockman.org

By the way, this book is not legal, medical, financial, psychological, horticultural, viticultural, marine biological, or any other professional advice. It is solely inspiration and motivation to my readers, conveying principles that I have seen to work well. The content is the opinion of the author. It is not eternal truth etched in stone (like the Ten Commandments). The author and publisher do not warranty or guarantee anything. Neither the author nor the publisher are liable for physical, psychological, emotional, financial, or commercial damages, including but not limited to special, incidental, consequential or other damages. You are responsible for your own choices, actions, and results.

Welcome to the world of being an adult.

ISBN: 978-1-7341146-8-3

To my wife.

Who has been telling me I've needed to get this workbook done for a couple years now.

Who has been the greatest gift I've ever received.

Who blesses me daily and who in spite of my terd-ness, still can't help but be attracted to me, flirt with me, and want me.

And she's loved me through some very tough times.

I can only write about marriage because I have excellent raw materials to work with.

TABLE OF CONTENTS

TABLE OF CONTENTS

00 / THIS IS ONE INTRODUCTION YOU DON'T WANT TO SKIP

PART ONE

01 / THE SEARCH FOR WHO YOU ARE

02 / GOD'S OPINION, YOUR REALITY

03 / WELCOME TO...YOU

/ PART 1 CAPSTONE

PART TWO

04 / STOP PANDERING FOR APPROVAL

05 / A MAN OF YOUR WORD, GOVERNED BY PRINCIPLE

06 / MASTER YOUR ALLEGIANCE

/ PART 2 CAPSTONE

PART THREE

07 / RECLAIMING YOUR FIRE

08 / HOW TO BE LEGENDARY

/ PART 3 CAPSTONE

MATT HALLOCK · DNA TACTICAL GUIDE · MAN WARRIOR KING

O

THIS IS ONE INTRODUCTION YOU DON'T WANT TO SKIP

ooo

O

MATT HALLOCK

MAN WARRIOR KING

000.   INTRODUCTION

INTRODUCTION

GETTING YOUR BEARINGS

In this life-change training we are going to invite the Holy Spirit to show us the honest, real truth about how we see ourselves, our lives, and even how we see Jesus.

We are going to honestly assess whether our current situation aligns with God's promises--His declaration over our lives. And, led by the Holy Spirit, we are going to expose false mindsets that have secretly kept us bound for far too long. Let's do this.

How would you describe your life in one paragraph? Ready...go!

In all honesty, when you consider the promises of Jesus and the experience of the early believers in the book of Acts...does your life as it currently stands match what you'd expect it to look like?

Do you even believe that your life should be a walking testimony of fulfilled promises? Is it even possible or appropriate for you to emulate the miraculous, victorious life you see in the book of Acts?

In *The DNA of a Man*, we start out by looking at the sorry state of Jerusalem that Nehemiah depicts for us in Nehemiah chapter one. Do you feel like that version of Jerusalem-- broken walls, burned out, in shame in disrepair? How so?

000. INTRODUCTION

FATHERS

01. **Describe your dad. How was/is your relationship with him? Do you trust him? Does he trust you? Do you experience action from him toward you that shows you--that proves to you--that he's in your corner?**

02. **What, if anything, do you blame your dad for? What, if anything, are you thankful to your dad for? How has your dad influenced your view of yourself and your view of God? Or, in other words, how has your dad influenced your relationship with yourself and with God?**

000. INTRODUCTION

VILLAINS

01. How does our culture portray masculinity as a negative? Where have you seen good manly qualities being attacked or undermined? What qualities are those? What masculine qualities do you think our culture needs that are in short supply in our day?

02. Where, other than the Bible, do you find your model for "a good man?" Anywhere?

SINNERS

The deepest, most fundamental, and arguably the most destructive attack on your masculinity comes from our common understanding of the Gospel itself.

Read again the section titled "Sinners" from the book's Introduction.

Take a walk somewhere outside by yourself. Take your time with this and ask God if what you have believed about yourself has been truly reflective of his heart, or if it has been simply your religious interpretation.

Have you seen yourself as a worthless sinner who is saved by grace? If so, how does this make you feel about yourself? How does it affect your confidence? Your leadership? Your strength and worth? Do you love yourself?

01.

000. INTRODUCTION

ROMANS LIFE CHANGE

In a minute, I'm going to have you read Romans chapter 8. As you read, ask the Holy Spirit to show you: Do you believe what you're reading? I mean REALLY believe it? Or do you find yourself saying, "Well yeah, but...?"

Or, "Of course this is true, if we take it in its historical context...?" Or, "I believe this is spiritually true, but it may not necessarily mean that I'll experience it?" Or, "This is true but mostly for when I 'die and go to heaven' ?"

BUT...before you read, I want you to get real with God. You are desperate for him to be real to you, so you must be ready to do the same.

Take some time to talk to him. Call it praying if you like, but we can get so locked into a religious routine when we think of "prayer." So if it helps, think of it as "letting him have it."

Give all your thoughts to him. Let them out. Tell him about your life and how you feel like a champion, a failure, a mediocre nobody, a conqueror, all of it. Tell him what you're thankful for and where you feel like he's deserted you.

Let tears flow. Yell. Pound your steering wheel. Cuss if you have to. Just get it out.

MATT HALLOCK

WWW.MANWARRIORKING.COM

000.　INTRODUCTION

ROMANS 8

For each section of scripture below, respond with the most jaw-dropping, earth-shattering truths that the Holy Spirit reveals to you.

What are you seeing that is such good news that you find it difficult to believe?

Remind yourself that these things are true of Jesus and of you...RIGHT NOW...not after you die someday.

ROMANS 8:1-11
Points to consider: Condemnation, freedom, Jesus and the Spirit in you

ROMANS 8:12-17
Points to consider: Your sonship, fear, your Father, your inheritance, your glory

ROMANS 8:18-30
Points to consider: Your glory, your adoption, the Spirit

ROMANS 8:31-39
Points to consider: Your advocate, your enemy, your security, your untouchability

MINDSET RESET

000.   INTRODUCTION

MODEL PRAYER
REWIRE MY BRAIN

Holy Spirit, Jesus said that you'd lead me into all truth. He promised me that you would reveal to me the things that he says and thinks, the things that the Father says and thinks."

"Would you do that right now? I'm laying down my prior understanding, my preconceived ideas about what Romans 8 means.

And I'm giving you permission to rewire my brain so that my thinking--my believing from my core--matches your heart.

I need you, and all the journaling, action-taking, and reading in the world won't do anything unless I encounter you, the living God. I am yours. Have your way with me right now."

01.   PART 1

PART ONE
A MAN OF IDENTITY

MATT HALLOCK   DNA TACTICAL GUIDE   WWW.MANWARRIORKING.COM

01

THE SEARCH FOR WHO YOU ARE

001

MATT HALLOCK · MAN WARRIOR KING

CHAPTER ONE
LIKE YOUR FATHER

One of the marks of sonship is that we very closely resemble our dad. We look like him. We sound like him. We smell like him. We have similar--or the SAME--mannerisms to his.

Now, that may or may not be good news to you, depending on how you feel about your dad.

That's beside the point.

Take a moment and jot down the things about your dad that you are proud to have in common with him.

Make a choice to focus only on any good you can think of. And ONLY good.

You also look, act, sound, smell, and behave like your Father, the creator of all things. The Dread Champion who fights for you and others who are oppressed and beat down.

Truthfully, I don't care if you don't believe that. Or if you think it's too good to be true.

His Word says it, so you have to either accept it as truth or deny his Word. Only you can make that choice.

If you KNEW that the spirit world trembled in fear when you enter the room, like they do in God's presence, how would it affect your life?

How would you carry yourself, feel about yourself, pray, dream, plan, fight....if you really GRASPED this?

001. THE SEARCH FOR WHO YOU ARE

IDENTITY: ITS ORIGINS AND YOUR INSECURITY

01. The need to "fit in" and be validated can drive men to search for identity in achievements, relationships, or external approval. Where have you let performance define your sense of worth? What happens emotionally when you succeed? What happens when you fail?

02. God declared Adam's identity before he did anything. You also were created in God's image to reflect His nature, yet many men struggle to see themselves as carrying His authority and power. What thoughts or beliefs are preventing you from fully embracing your God-given identity?

001. THE SEARCH FOR WHO YOU ARE

A MAN WITH NO IDENTITY

01. **Fear:** In what areas of your marriage or life do you operate from fear instead of strength? How has fear shaped your decisions, especially in how you interact with your wife?

02. **Dependence:** Where do you depend on external circumstances—such as your wife's mood, career success, or people's opinions—to feel secure? How would your life change if your confidence came from God alone?

001.   THE SEARCH FOR WHO YOU ARE

03.   **Depression: Have you ever felt a deep lack of worth or purpose? What have you tried to use to "fix" this feeling, and why hasn't it worked?**

04.   **Smallness: Have you been living "small" in your marriage, work, or faith—hesitating to take action, avoiding risks, or holding back your voice? What would it take for you to start stepping up as the man you were created to be?**

001.   THE SEARCH FOR WHO YOU ARE

THE CULPRIT

01. When you look at your marriage, career, and personal struggles, do you tend to see yourself as a victim of circumstances, or as a man who has contributed to his situation? What would it look like to take full ownership, like Nehemiah, instead of waiting for someone else to fix it?

02. In what ways have you "sat in the corner, babying your wounds" instead of stepping into your God-given authority as a man? What is one specific area where you need to stop making excuses and start acting in strength?

JEREMIAH LIFE CHANGE

Next I want you to look at Jeremiah chapter 1. Pay close attention to the way God speaks about and to Jeremiah, and notice Jeremiah's immediate reaction to what God is saying.

Who is saying the positive things?

Who is saying the negative?

Pretty eye-opening to look at this chapter through that lens. Isn't it amazing how you and I can hear so many negative thoughts about ourselves, and how we most often attribute those to what God must also think about us?

Couple that with the fact that a large portion of church culture will openly tell us that we shouldn't think too highly of ourselves.

"We aren't all that great, after all."

But in Jeremiah 1, notice just how highly God thinks of this man, and the magnitude and honor involved in the calling that God has placed on his life.

You too are a Jeremiah.

This word was written for you as an example of how God deals with you. Let him speak to you personally in it.

000.   THE SEARCH FOR WHO YOU ARE

JEREMIAH 1

For each section of scripture below, respond with the most jaw-dropping, earth-shattering truths that the Holy Spirit reveals to you.

What are you seeing about your own calling, worth, and the state of your inner world?

Remember to ask the Holy Spirit to apply the Scripture uniquely to you, to take it from a distant historical truth, to his specific message to YOU.

JEREMIAH 1:1-5
Points to consider: Your calling, before you were born, God's care

JEREMIAH 1:6-10
Points to consider: Your objections to God's good words, His response, fear, deliverance, His words in you, your authority

000. THE SEARCH FOR WHO YOU ARE

JEREMIAH 1:11-19
Points to consider: Your mission, your strength, your enemies, your Advocate and Warrior

REFLECTION AND GROUP DISCUSSION
- Where have you argued with God about your identity instead of simply accepting what He has declared over you?

- Jeremiah felt unqualified, yet God didn't lower the calling—He raised Jeremiah up to meet it. What area of your life is God calling you to step into, even if you don't feel ready?

- If God told you that your worth was determined before you were even born, why do you still let failures or weaknesses define you?

- What would shift in your life if you stopped making excuses and fully embraced your God-given identity?

MODEL PRAYER
CUTTING TIES

Father, I repent of walking through life as though I have no identity. I repent of believing that I'm not worth much to you, or to the world for that matter.

Father, I renounce living in fear, elevating my enemies above you, my Ally.

I renounce dependence on circumstances and people to give me my meaning, fulfillment, and general sense of worth and well-being.

I renounce depression and refuse to ever agree with it ever again. My inheritance from you is joy and peace, lightness and gladness, victory over all darkness.

And lastly, Father, I repent of living small. I cut all ties with smallness of mind, smallness of behavior, smallness of presence. I will be a man who walks in purpose, power, and confidence, as you designed me to, in Jesus' name. Amen.

O

GOD'S OPINION, YOUR REALITY

002

2

MATT HALLOCK

MAN WARRIOR KING

CHAPTER TWO
SPINNING YOUR WHEELS

Chapter 2 of the book starts out setting the stage for the arrival of Gideon, God's chosen deliverer during a time when Israel was "laid waste" and "brought very low."

Are there any areas of your own life that currently feel like they've been laid to waste? Or brought extremely low?

Do you feel like--in this area--no matter what you do, how hard you work, you just keep on spinning your wheels? Has it caused you to blame God?

What area is this and how does it make you feel?

When we first see Gideon, he's in hiding, for fear that he'll be caught trying to thresh wheat without the approval of his land's captors.

Living in hiding makes perfect sense. When a man is under attack, constantly beat down by life, made to feel like his every effort is futile, worthless, and not enough to meet the challenge at hand, hiding is only natural.

But you and I aren't natural any longer.

We are SUPERNATURAL.

So, where are you walking through life afraid? Afraid of others? Afraid of bills? Afraid of God? Afraid of the future?

Ask the Holy Spirit to show you.

GIDEON'S CALL: YOUR EMPOWERMENT

01. Where in your life have you allowed fear to dictate your decisions? What would change if you stopped empowering your fears and instead stood firm in the identity God has given you?

02. Have you ever let your past failures or current struggles convince you that you are not truly a strong, valuable, powerful man of God? How have you formed an opinion of yourself based on your performance rather than on what God says?

YOUR IDENTITY THE KEY TO LIFE CHANGE

01. If it's true that your performance means nothing about your worth, how does that bring you hope, inner freedom, and a surge of joy? Have you previously considered your performance as the measuring stick?

02. How do you typically see yourself? Are you proud of who you are? Are you glad to be you? Are you ashamed to be you? If God disagrees with your own self-assessment, is it possible your negative thoughts are sin?

002.   GOD'S OPINION, YOUR REALITY

03. **If Gideon's experience and behavior flowed from the narrative that was spoken over him, what narrative is being spoken over you? By yourself? By others? By God?**

04. **Identity is more powerful than circumstances. What circumstances in your life have you simply accepted as "your lot" without checking to see if they line up with God's promises in his Word? What would happen if you refused to accept ANY event or circumstance that went against ANY of his promises?**

WHOSE VOICE WILL YOU CHOOSE

01. **Becoming a Kingdom Man:** Jesus said that the kingdom of heaven is taken by force. In what area of your life have you been passive, waiting for permission, instead of boldly advancing in the calling God has given you? What step will you take this week to step into your strength?

02. Think of a time when you didn't speak up, but knew that you should have. Repent of it in writing here. Thank God for forgiving you (again, in writing). Now, ask him for an opportunity to rock the boat again in the near future, where YOU will be the one to speak up for the sake of good.

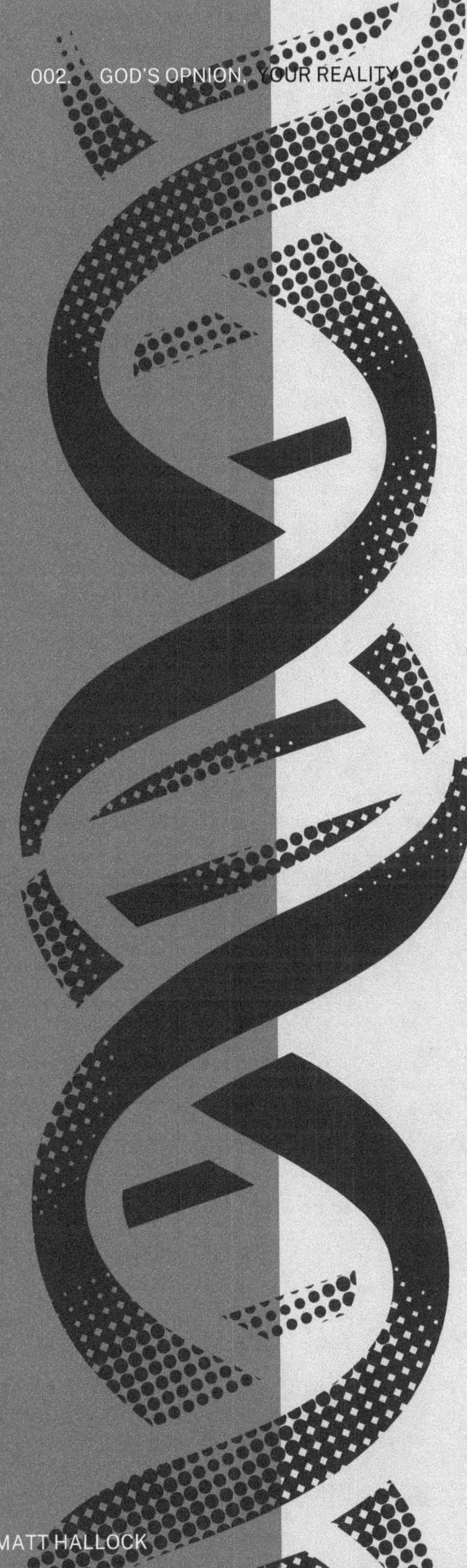

GIDEON LIFE CHANGE

For this chapter, I want you to analyze the conversation between Gideon and God for yourself. Don't settle for simply reading my quotations of it in *DNA*.

The thing that is so powerful about this moment in Gideon's life is that it shows just how NON-religious God is. He has no problem overlooking the weaknesses and flaws of Gideon to call him to a higher level of existence.

He KNOWS the masculine strength and confidence that he instilled into Gideon since before the womb.

He KNOWS the calling on his life to rise up in strength and deliver a whole nation from the grip of oppression.

And THAT is what he cares about. Not about the fear, the hiding, the arguing, the self-deprecation.

Do you know why he doesn't even seem to notice those things?

Because of Isaiah 43:45. He is the one who blots out our transgressions and remembers our sins NO MORE.

He legally took care of your weaknesses and shortcomings through the death, burial, and resurrection of Jesus, so now he only thinks about your Identity. Excellent news.

002.   GOD'S OPINION, YOUR REALITY

JUDGES 6

For each section of scripture below, respond with the most jaw-dropping, earth-shattering truths that the Holy Spirit reveals to you.

What are you seeing about your own calling, worth, and what God just might think about you?

Remember to ask the Holy Spirit to apply the Scripture uniquely to you, to take it from a distant historical truth, to his specific message to YOU.

JUDGES 6:1-6

Points to consider: Your enemies, your failures, oppression, spinning wheels

JUDGES 6:7-10

Points to consider: Consequences of your thinking, God's rescue, crying out to Him

002. GOD'S OPINION, YOUR REALITY

JUDGES 6:11-18
Points to consider: God's decree, Gideon's self-deprecation, God's response, the battle of narratives

REFLECTION AND GROUP DISCUSSION
- Where in your life have you believed the lie that you are too weak, too broken, or too insignificant to do something great?

- Gideon's transformation began when he chose to agree with God instead of his fears. What would shift in your life if you made that same choice?

- When God calls you strong, capable, and powerful, do you argue with Him like Gideon did? Why?

- What does Gideon's story reveal about the connection between identity and action?

MODEL PRAYER
NEW NARRATIVE

Father, please teach me how to live my life from a totally different starting point. Where I am governed by what you say about me, not by how I feel, what others think, or what's happening around me.

Teach me to cling to the incredible things you say about me, even when I'm still stuck in my muck, my weakness, my failing, my sin.

I'm sorry for thinking that I had to clean myself up in order to get close to you. I've believed a lie.

Truly, what you want is for me to hear what you call me, humbly accept it, even if it sounds too good to be true, and in so doing draw close to you where you'll completely transform me so my weaknesses all melt off.

I choose to yield my allegiance to you...not to hell and its narrative.

Thank you for freeing me, in Jesus's name. Amen

03

003

MATT HALLOCK　　　　　　　　　　　　　　　　　　　　　　　　MAN WARRIOR KING

CHAPTER THREE
YOUR SONSHIP

Chapter three is all about fleshing out what EXACTLY your God-given Identity truly is.

As the book argues, first and foremost, you are a son. A son of the Father of all things. A son of the one who rules all of the heavens and the earth to the ends of the universe.

If this is the case, then why do so many of us Christians live our lives feeling like orphans? As though we are completely alone in the earth? Struggling to get by.

Do you live your days typically feeling more like a son who belongs? Or an orphan on the streets?

The notion that you and I are sons is not necessarily new. Anyone who's been a Christian for a short amount of time is familiar with the concept that we are now children of God.

But think about the first part of this chapter in the book. My sonship meant that I had free, unhindered access to everything that was my dad's domain.

And I had honor and recognition because of HIM.

So think about your sonship in terms of its legal ramifications. According to Scripture, can you think of the legal consequences for your being God's son?

What about your legal inheritance? Your legal authority? The power that you have a right to carry?

WHAT YOUR IDENTITY MEANS FOR YOU

01. Romans 8 says that all of creation is waiting for the sons of God to be revealed. If the entire world benefits when you step into your full identity, what is being held back because you haven't fully embraced it? What specific impact do you believe God wants you to have, and what is one way you can begin to take action on that today?

02. If you fully embraced the reality that you are a son of God—with unrestricted access to His power, love, and provision—how would that change the way you carry yourself in your marriage, parenting, or leadership? How would you "roam the halls with confidence?" What is one specific way you can walk in that confidence today?

OKAY, BUT WHAT IS MY IDENTITY?

01. **A RIGHTEOUS SAINT:** How would your confidence, actions, and relationships change if you truly saw yourself as a righteous saint rather than a sinner barely hanging on by grace? Where have you unknowingly embraced self-degradation instead of the honor, worth, and authority God has given you? Why do you suppose we've been conditioned to be so sin focused, when Romans tells us to be righteousness focused?

02. **LIKE JESUS, FULL OF GLORY, AUTHORITY, AND POWER:** Does this one offend you at all? Why? What if playing small and looking down on yourself is actually pride...not humility? Describe the excitement you'd feel if Jesus came to you and told you himself that he's handing off his power and authority to YOU until he comes back? What would you do differently?

03. **I HAVE A RIGHT TO HEALTH:** If sickness has no place in your identity as a son of God, what would it look like to stop "making peace" with physical struggles and start treating your health as a right, not a hope? In what ways have you unconsciously accepted sickness as normal rather than something Jesus already paid to remove?

04. **I AM DESIGNED TO PROSPER:** How does this notion hold up against Scripture? There are many out there who attack the "health and wealth" gospel….what about you? Can you find promises where God says he wants his children to be poor and lacking things? If God says he wants us to prosper, then where does the aversion to riches in the church come from?

003.   WELCOME TO...YOU

05.
I AM FREE AND VICTORIOUS: Are you aware that you are free from sin, even if you've sinned earlier today? Are you living in the reality that you are immediately clean the moment you repent? More than that, God forgets it all...all the sin! What sins do you need to forgive yourself for and choose to finally let go of?

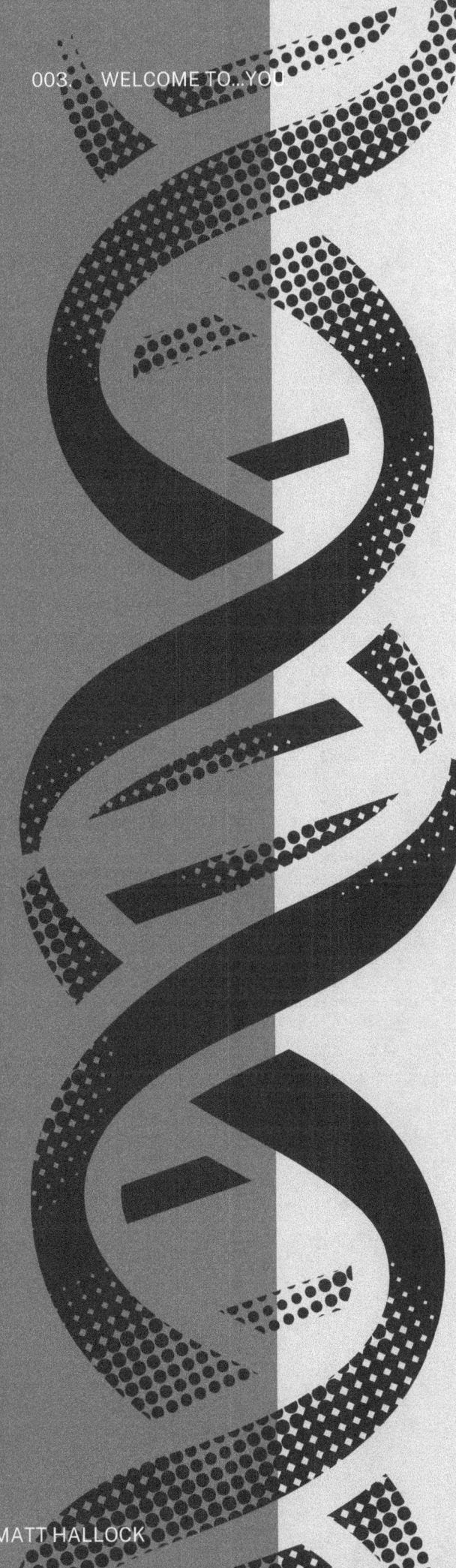

NEHEMIAH LIFE CHANGE

The final section of Chapter 3 depicts the kind of man that we all likely want to be:

Emotionally strong.

Resilient...not a quitter.

Full of value, always blessing others around him.

A master of himself and his space.

Not nice.

Watchful, vigilant, protector.

Anti-fragile, in other words, impervious to pain.

He believes what God says, at face value.

Incredible right? This type of manhood is yours too. It's already in you. You just have conditioned yourself to believe lies about you and so you don't know that this is truly who you are.

For this chapter, I want you to dig into the story of Nehemiah. He was a man who didn't wait for permission to take action. He was emotionally strong. Absolutely not "nice." And he dove into conflict head first.

Ask the Holy Spirit to plant these seeds in you as you dig in.

003.   WELCOME TO...YOU

NEHEMIAH

For each section of scripture below, respond with the most jaw-dropping, earth-shattering truths that the Holy Spirit reveals to you.

What are you seeing about your call to take initiative, to stand up and be vigilant over your life and your domain?

Remember to ask the Holy Spirit to apply the Scripture uniquely to you, to take it from a distant historical truth, to his specific message to YOU.

NEHEMIAH 1:1-11
Points to consider: Taking ownership over the problems you see, Nehemiah's repentance, holding God to his word, overcoming fear

NEHEMIAH 2:1-8
Points to consider: Taking initiative, humility, creating a vision and a plan, favor from the king

003. WELCOME TO...YOU

NEHEMIAH 2:9-20
Points to consider: Being vigilant, thorough and excellent in what you do, Nehemiah's faith and optimism, his ability to inspire others through that faith

NEHEMIAH 4:1-23
Points to consider: Facing opposition, resilience, faith in God's promises over our circumstances, when God's will doesn't match your circumstances

MINDSET RESET

REFLECTION AND GROUP DISCUSSION
- What obstacles in your life have you wrongly interpreted as signs to quit? How does Nehemiah challenge that mindset?

- How did Nehemiah balance faith in God with taking personal responsibility? How can you do the same?

- What does Nehemiah's leadership teach you about ruling over your space and bringing order?

- How can you embody his boldness in your own calling and relationships?

MODEL PRAYER
STEPPING IN

Father, I choose today to step fully into the identity You have given me. No more hesitating. No more waiting for permission from life, circumstances, or others to become the man You say I am. You have already called me strong, capable, and equipped—so I will walk in that truth, not in the lies of my past or the doubts in my mind.

Like Nehemiah, I refuse to back down when obstacles come. I will not interpret resistance as a sign to quit, but as confirmation that I am advancing in the right direction. When life tries to shut me down, I will press forward in the power You have placed within me.

I reject the mindset of passivity and smallness. I will not live apologetically or let the opinions of others define me. I am not here to blend in—I am here to build, to lead, and to bring Your kingdom into my world.

Father, help me see myself as You see me. Give me the courage to own my space, rule with strength, and love with confidence. I choose to walk in boldness today, fully stepping into all that You have already declared over me.

Thank You for making me a son, a leader, a warrior. I will not live beneath my calling.
In Jesus' name, Amen.

A MAN OF IDENTITY
PART ONE
CAPSTONE

MATT HALLOCK

MAN WARRIOR KING

A MAN OF IDENTITY
- PART ONE CAPSTONE -

ACCORDING TO MY FATHER, I AM...

In this exercise, you're going to evaluate a very big number of "I am" statements, derived directly from Scripture. The purpose of this exercise has several facets.

One, I want you to practice simply **receiving for YOU** what is written. In the mundane routine of "morning devotions" we can end up glossing over verses that are meant to pick you up out of low and small living. Instead, we see them and immediately dismiss them as metaphorical, for someone else, or simply too good to be true for you, because there's no way you qualify.

Or, you may see a verse and have a host of reasons why that verse can't mean what it actually says. The problem is, your reasons are usually inferior, based on experiences you've had, circumstances you're in, or "wisdom" someone else has taught you.

But now, I want you to lay all that aside, and truly SEE what these verses are saying to YOU. See what your Father thinks about you. And who you truly are. No dismissals, no excuses, and no disqualifiers.

Ask for the Holy Spirit's guidance, that he would highlight the specific verses that he's wanting to focus on with you at this time in your life. They are all yours. But which ones does he know you need in order to heal in some way, to uplevel to the next version of yourself, or to begin to win in ways you haven't yet?

On the page following the list, you'll see spaces to write 10 of these statements. If you want to write more, use more paper. But write out at least 10. And yes, DO write them yourself. Simply reading them is nowhere near as important as OWNING them through your writing.

Be a doer of the word, not just a hearer. So write!

Please note: I cannot take credit for compiling this list. I found it years ago and have kept it ever since. The source is unknown.

A MAN OF IDENTITY
- PART ONE CAPSTONE -
ACCORDING TO MY FATHER, I AM...

I have been healed. (Isaiah 53:5)

I am the salt of the earth. (Matthew 5:13)

I am the light of the world. (Matthew 5:14)

I am commissioned to make disciples. (Matthew 28:19,20)

I am a child of God. (John 1:12)

I have eternal life. (John 10:27)

I have been given peace. (John 14:27)

I am part of the true vine, a channel of Christ's life. (John 15:1,5)

I am clean. (John 15:3)

I am Christ's friend. (John 15:15)

I am chosen and appointed by Christ to bear His fruit. (John 15:16)

I have been given glory. (John 17:22)

I have been justified...completely forgiven and made righteous.
(Romans 5:1)

I died with Christ and died to the power of sin's rule over my life.
(Romans 6:1-6)

I am a slave of righteousness. (Romans 6:18)

I am free from sin and enslaved to God. (Romans 6:22)

I am free forever from condemnation. (Romans 8:1)

I am a son of God; God is spiritually my Father. (Romans 8:14, 15 Galatians 3:26; 4:6)

I am a joint heir with Christ, sharing His inheritance with Him (Romans 8:17)

I am more than a conqueror through Christ, who loves me. (Romans 8:37)

I have faith. (Romans 12:3)

I have been sanctified and called to holiness. (1 Corinthians 1:2)

I have been given grace in Christ Jesus. (1Corinthians 1:4)

I have been placed into Christ, by God's doing. (1 Corinthians 1:30)

I have received the Spirit of God into my life that I might know the
things feely given to me by God. (1 Corinthians 2:12)

I have been given the mind of Christ. (1 Corinthians 2:16)

A MAN OF IDENTITY
- PART ONE CAPSTONE -
ACCORDING TO MY FATHER, I AM...

I am a temple...a dwelling place...of God. His Spirit and His life dwell in me. (1 Corinthians 3:16; 6:19)

I am united to the Lord and am one spirit with Him. (1 Corinthians 6:17)

I am bought with a price; I am not my own; I belong to God.
(1 Corinthians 6:19,20; 7:23)

I am called. (1 Corinthians 7:17)

I am a member of Christ's Body.
(1 Corinthians 12:27; Ephesians 5:30)

I am victorious through Jesus Christ.
(1 Corinthians 15:57)

I have been established, anointed and sealed by God in Christ, and I have been given to the Holy Spirit as a pledge guaranteeing my inheritance to come.
(2 Corinthians 1:21; Ephesians 1:13,14)

I am led by God in triumphal procession. (2 Corinthians 2:14)

I am to God the fragrance of Christ among those who are being saved and those who are perishing.
(2 Corinthians 2:15)

I am being changed into the likeness of Christ. (2 Corinthians 3:18)

Since I have died, I no longer live for myself, but for Christ.
(2 Corinthians 5:14,15)

I am a new creation. (2 Corinthians 5:17)

I am reconciled to God and am a minister of reconciliation. (2 Corinthians 5:18,19)

I have been made righteous.
(2 Corinthians 5:21)

I am given strength in exchange for weakness. (2 Corinthians 12:10)

I have been crucified with Christ and it is no longer I who live, but Christ lives in me. The life I am now living is Christ's life. (Galatians 2:20)

I am a son of God and one in Christ. (Galatians 3:26, 28)

I am Abraham's seed...an heir of the promise. (Galatians 3:29)

I am an heir of God since I am a son of God. (Galatians 4:6,7)

I am a saint. (Ephesians 1:1; ! Corinthians 1:2; Philippians 1:1; Colossians 1:2)

I have been blessed with every spiritual blessing. (Ephesians 1:3)

A MAN OF IDENTITY
- PART ONE CAPSTONE -
ACCORDING TO MY FATHER, I AM...

I was chosen in Christ before the foundation of the world to be holy and am without blame before Him. (Ephesians 1:4)

I was predestined...determined by God...to be adopted as God's son. (Ephesians 1:5)

I have been redeemed and forgiven, and I am a recipient of His lavish grace. (Ephesians 1:7)

I have been sealed with the Holy Spirit. (Ephesians 1:13)

I have been made alive together with Christ. (Ephesians 2:5)

I have been raised up and seated with Christ in heaven. (Ephesians 2:6)

I am God's workmanship...His handiwork...born anew in Christ to do His work. (Ephesians 2:10)

I have direct access to God through the Spirit. (Ephesians 2:18)

I am a fellow citizen with the rest of God's family. (Ephesians 2:19)

I may approach God with boldness, freedom, and confidence. (Eph. 3:12)

I am righteous and holy. (Ephesians 2:24)

I am a citizen of heaven, seated in heaven right now. (Philippians 3:20 Ephesians 2:6)

I am capable. (Philippians 4:13)

I have been rescued from the domain of Satan's rule and transferred to the kingdom of Christ. (Colossians 1:13)

I have been redeemed and forgiven of all my sins. The debt against me has been cancelled. (Colossians 1:14)

I am blameless and free from accusation. (Colossians 1:22)

Christ Himself is in me. (Colossians 1:27)

I am firmly rooted in Christ and am now being built up in Him. (Col. 2:7)

I have been made complete in Christ. (Colossians 2:10)

I have been spiritually circumcised. My old unregenerate nature has been removed. (Colossians 2:11)

I have been buried, raised, and made alive with Christ. (Colossians 2:12,13)

I died with Christ and I have been raised up with Christ. My life is now hidden with Christ in God. Christ is now my life. (Colossians 1:1-4)

I am an expression of the life of Christ because He is my life. (Colossians 3:4)

A MAN OF IDENTITY
- PART ONE CAPSTONE -
ACCORDING TO MY FATHER, I AM...

I am chosen of God, holy and dearly loved. (Col. 3:12; 1 Thessalonians 1:4)

I am a son of light and not of darkness. (1 Thessalonians 5:5)

I have been given a spirit of power, love, and self-discipline. (2 Timothy 1:7)

I have been saved and set apart according to God's doing. (2 Timothy 1:9; Titus 3:5)

Because I am sanctified and am one with the Sanctifier, He is not ashamed to call me brother. (Hebrews 2:11)

I am a holy partaker of a heavenly calling. (Hebrews 3:1)

I have the right to come boldly before the throne of God to find mercy and grace in a time of need. (Hebrews 4:16)

I have been born again. (1 Peter 1:23)

I am one of God's living stones, being built up in Christ as a spiritual house. (1 Peter 2:5)

I am a member of a chosen race, a royal priesthood, a holy nation, a people for God's own possession. (1 Peter 2:9,10)

I am an alien and stranger to this world in which I temporarily live. (1 Peter 2:11)

I am an enemy of the devil. (1 Peter 2:11)

I have been given exceedingly great and precious promises by God by which I am a partaker of God's divine nature. (2 Peter 1:4)

I am forgiven on the account of Jesus' name. (1 John 2:12)

I am anointed by God. (1 John 2:27)

I am a child of God and I will resemble Christ when He returns. (1 John 3:1,2)

I am loved. (1 John 4:10)

I am like Christ. (1 John 4:10)

I have life. (1 John 5:12)

I am born of God, and the evil one...the devil...cannot touch me. (1 John 5:18)

I have been redeemed. (Revelation 5:9)

A MAN OF IDENTITY
- PART ONE CAPSTONE -
ACCORDING TO MY FATHER, I AM...

01.

02.

03.

04.

05.

06.

07.

08.

09.

10.

A MAN OF IDENTITY
- PART ONE CAPSTONE -

YOUR PERSONAL IDENTITY STATEMENT

In the spaces below, take some time to think through who you are as God's son, as a man, as a husband, and as a dad. Write down bulleted "I am" statements that capture the essence of who you want and intend to be. These are not necessarily quotes from Scripture. They are unique to you and your desires.

Note: None of these is to be negative in any way. They are all positive statements about you at your best. Why? Because that's how God created you and how he sees you. *If you need more space, use some more paper.*

01 - SON

02 - MAN

03 - HUSBAND

04 - DAD

02.   PART 2

PART TWO
A MAN OF PRINCIPLE

MATT HALLOCK · DNA TACTICAL GUIDE · MAN WARRIOR KING

O

STOP PANDERING FOR APPROVAL

004

4

MATT HALLOCK   MAN WARRIOR KING

004.   STOP PANDERING FOR APPROVAL

CHAPTER FOUR

EMBRACING PRINCIPLE

I started Chapter Four in *DNA* by recounting the adventure of me and two brothers attacking enemy combatants and fleeing for our lives when we were nearly caught.

(In the book, of course, we know this was merely water-ballooning cars as they drove past.)

And you learned that I abandoned one of my brothers-in-arms that day to take the fall.

Lack of Principle.

Based on what you know of Scripture, why is living by Principle so valuable, and even required?

Something important to note is that God himself found it crucial to immortalize his own principles in writing. He does not simply wing it through history. Rather, he is intentional, and he carries himself with excellence.

Take a moment here to ask the Holy Spirit for his help. If you feel as though you've let unintentionality take over your life in any big or small way, ask Him to remove that from you.

Thank him for filling you with his character, his intention, his excellence.

Declare to yourself that you ARE indeed a man of excellence. Principle will henceforth guide you, not circumstance, not others' opinions, not your feelings.

004. STOP PANDERING FOR APPROVAL

PRINCIPLE STEMS FROM IDENTITY

01. When you walk into a new environment—whether at work, church, or a social setting—do you instinctively take a "pulse check" before being yourself? How would your presence shift if you walked into every room already anchored in unshakable principles rather than waiting for external validation?

02. God gave Adam a clear choice—follow an external, unshakable principle or be swayed by the urgency of the moment. Where in your life have you allowed circumstances, emotions, or others' opinions to dictate your choices rather than governing yourself by strong internal principles? How can you correct this today?

HUSBANDING WITHOUT PRINCIPLE

01. Adam waited and followed rather than lead with strength. Are there areas in your life where you've subtly adopted a posture of waiting for permission rather than taking decisive action based on your principles? How can you step into bold leadership today, independent of external approval?

02. If an outside observer watched your daily interactions with your wife, would they say that your leadership is guided by strong, God-given principles, or by the shifting tides of her emotions and approval? What specific step can you take today to lead your wife from a place of conviction rather than reaction to her mood?

03. Are you loving your wife as a man who is anchored in God's authority, or are you modifying your behavior to avoid upsetting her? How would your marriage change if you stopped aiming to 'keep her happy' and instead committed to leading her with strength, love, and truth—regardless of how she responds in the moment?

04. What if "Happy wife, happy life" is a lie? What if it sets us up to lose our wife's respect and affection over time? In what way was Adam living by that mantra in the garden, rather than as a confident secure man? Have you been guilty of the same behavior? If so, what are you going to do about it now that you know?

004. STOP PANDERING FOR APPROVAL

ADAM LIFE CHANGE

In the early chapters of Genesis, we see Adam fail to lead Eve with principle. He remained passive when it mattered most, and he allowed external influences to dictate his actions—all of which are classic signs of lack of Principle.

This is made even more tragic because he was given, directly from God, a crystal clear--and extremely--simple set of principles to live by.

"Don't eat from the one tree." That was it!

But he instead allowed the external circumstances of the serpent initiating a conversation, his wife going along with the evil scheme, and her invitation for him to join her---

He let all these override his God-given code of conduct. And we know the deadly ramifications.

What if the ramifications for you when you don't live by Principle are every bit as toxic, dangerous, and harmful to yourself and your wife?

As we dig into Adam's story, ask the Holy Spirit to awaken you to the danger of passivity, and being too agreeable.

Ask him to help you to grow in the virtue of DISAGREEABILITY.

MATT HALLOCK

004.   STOP PANDERING FOR APPROVAL

ADAM

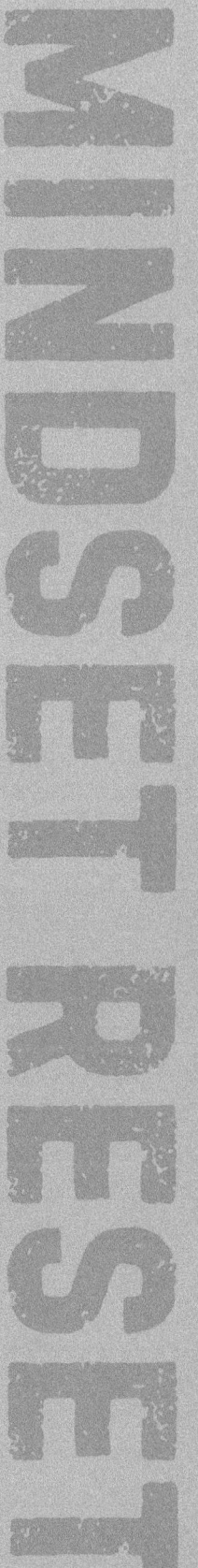

For each section of scripture below, respond with the most jaw-dropping, earth-shattering truths that the Holy Spirit reveals to you.

What are you seeing about your own tendency toward either Principle or passivity? Is it possible some of this is at work in your marriage?

Remember to ask the Holy Spirit to apply the Scripture uniquely to you, to take it from a distant historical truth, to his specific message to YOU.

GENESIS 2:15-25

Points to consider: God's command to Adam, the bliss and harmony of marriage as it was intended, the sensuality of marriage, the goodness of Principle

GENESIS 3:1-13

Points to consider: Adam being overcome by Eve's sexiness (possibly), his desire to keep her happy so he could get what he wants from her, "Happy wife, happy life"

004.   STOP PANDERING FOR APPROVAL

GENESIS 3:14-24
Points to consider: The result of marital disharmony, the woman trying to lead the man, the man needing now to toil, eviction from bliss

ADDITIONAL POINT: Jesus came to free us from the curse, so even though the results of our dysfunction are seen in Genesis 3, you and I now have the ability to rise above the curse through Jesus, and to get back the bliss and harmony we saw in Genesis 2.

REFLECTION AND GROUP DISCUSSION
- Where in your life have you allowed external voices—whether from your wife, culture, or fear—to override the principles you know you should be leading from?

- Adam remained silent when he should have spoken truth. Where have you been passive when your leadership was needed?

- After his failure, Adam blamed Eve instead of taking responsibility. How have you responded when things have gone wrong in your marriage or life? Have you owned your role, or have you subtly blamed others?

- What would Adam's story have looked like if he had chosen to stand firm in God's command? What can you learn from that?

MODEL PRAYER
TAKING IT BACK

Father, for too long, I have allowed circumstances, opinions, and fear to dictate how I lead, how I speak, and how I act. I have hesitated when I should have stood firm. I have remained silent when I should have spoken truth. I have followed when You called me to lead. Today, I take it back.

I take back my responsibility to live as a Man of Principle—anchored in truth, unwavering in conviction, and governed by Your voice above all others. I refuse to let passivity or approval-seeking define me. I will step forward boldly, guided by the principles You have written on my heart.

I take back my authority in my marriage. No longer will I wait to see how my wife feels before deciding how I will act. I will love her with strength, with truth, and with leadership—not out of fear, but out of the calling You have placed on me as a husband.

I take back my voice. Like Adam, I have been silent when I should have spoken. I will no longer shrink back, afraid of conflict or discomfort. I will speak with wisdom, with love, and with courage.

I take back my confidence. No longer will I allow my sense of self to be dictated by shifting emotions or external validation. My security comes from You alone, and I will carry myself as a man who knows who he is and what he stands for.

Today, I take it all back.

In Jesus' name, Amen.

05

A MAN OF YOUR WORD, GOVERNED BY PRINCIPLE

MATT HALLOCK

MAN WARRIOR KING

CHAPTER FIVE

FINDING THE SWEET SPOT

In Chapter Five of *DNA*, I discuss a couple of potential pitfalls that you and I can come up against on our journey of growing into Men of Principle.

One, the more "secular" problem of being our own captain without a King. Right? We know this. Jesus is our King, and so we have the honor of living life in submission to and in partnership with Him.

So, any code we live by, should be in alignment with his desires too, right?

Can you think of any times you've lived by a code that was your own? Not involving him at all? How did that work out?

The second pitfall, which I would say is quite a bit more common among Christian men, is to take the opposite stance: "I'm not the captain of my ship AT ALL."

This one is sneaky, deceptive, looks holy and right in light of the fact that we serve our King Jesus and submit to him.

But the truth is, too many of us have succumbed to holy-passivity, a way of life in which I have zero ownership, ability, or responsibility, because it's all "in his hands," or "in his timing," or "if it's his will."

God WANTS a powerful relationship with you, where you have input, opinions, desires, and agency.

Ask the Holy Spirit about this...what is he telling you?

THE INCOMPLETE, DEATH-INDUCING PICTURE

01. **Where in your life have you mistaken compliance for conviction?**
Have you been following certain "Christian" behaviors because they are expected of you, rather than because they are driven by a fiery love for God and a deep sense of purpose? How would your faith and leadership look different if you truly lived from a place of divine passion rather than religious obligation?

02. **How has the church's incomplete message of "just be good" stripped you of your fire and strength?**
In what ways has a passive, overly rule-driven version of Christian masculinity influenced your marriage, your parenting, or your leadership? Have you ever felt like you had to suppress your natural aggression, drive, or risk-taking because you thought it wasn't "Christian"? What has been the result?

005.   A MAN OF YOUR WORD, GOVERNED BY PRINCIPLE

03. **What areas of your life reveal that you have been living as a "religious corpse" instead of a man fully alive?**
Where have you settled for lukewarm, passive Christianity instead of the radical, adventurous, and bold faith Jesus modeled? What would change if you embraced your God-given fire instead of fearing it?

04. **Where have you let fear of offense or social disapproval dictate your choices rather than unwavering principle?**
Have you ever held back from speaking truth, taking a stand, or defending what's right because you didn't want to upset someone? How does this hesitation impact your ability to lead, protect, and provide in the way God designed you to?

005.   A MAN OF YOUR WORD, GOVERNED BY PRINCIPLE

05.
What's the difference between living as a rule-follower and living as a man whose actions stem from deep-rooted conviction?
What would shift in your faith, your marriage, and your work if your actions weren't just about checking boxes, but were instead driven by an unshakable inner compass?

06.
In what ways have you been trained to be "safe" instead of dangerous for the Kingdom?
Have you been conditioned to avoid conflict, play small, and stay within the lines of what is expected? What would it look like for you to become a dangerous man for the Kingdom—one who shakes things up, takes ground, and refuses to live passively?

THE COMPLETE PICTURE: SLAVERY AND RULERSHIP

01. **What does it look like for you to submit to Jesus while also walking in your God-given authority?**
Have you ever wrestled with the tension between surrendering to God and stepping into your own rulership as a son? How can you better embrace both—becoming a man who fully submits and fully leads?

02. **What principles are you currently living by—and are they ones you have chosen with Jesus or ones you've simply absorbed from culture, family, or church?**
Have you ever consciously decided what values and truths will govern your life, or have you just gone with the flow of what you were taught? What would it look like for you to intentionally choose your principles alongside Jesus?

005.   A MAN OF YOUR WORD, GOVERNED BY PRINCIPLE

Where have you hesitated to take initiative in life because you believed you couldn't be trusted?
Have you been waiting for external permission—whether from God, your wife, or others—before you step into leadership? How does Romans 5 challenge that hesitation, showing that God has already entrusted you to reign in life?

03.

What's one area of your life where you've been hesitant to ask "whatever you wish" from God?
John 15:7 says that if we abide in Jesus, we can ask anything and it will be done for us. Have you placed limits on what you believe you can ask for or receive? What's holding you back from living fully in that promise?

04.

005.   A MAN OF YOUR WORD, GOVERNED BY PRINCIPLE

How would your decision-making change if you fully trusted that God likes and honors your desires?
Psalm 37:4 says that when we delight in the Lord, He gives us the desires of our heart. Have you ever dismissed or suppressed your own desires out of fear that they aren't "holy enough"? How would your life change if you trusted that God wants you to dream and to pursue those dreams?

05.

In what ways have you lived like a "servant" instead of a "friend" of Jesus?
Jesus said in John 15:15 that he no longer calls us servants but friends. Do you relate to Jesus as a close friend who trusts and empowers you, or as a distant master whose approval you must earn? What needs to shift in your relationship with him?

06.

005. A MAN OF YOUR WORD, GOVERNED BY PRINCIPLE

HUSBANDS OF OUR WORD

What would your marriage look like if you were a man of unwavering conviction rather than a man who adjusts to his wife's mood?
Imagine a version of yourself who lives each day rooted in unshakable principles, where your actions remain consistent regardless of her approval or disapproval. How would this shift the dynamic between you and your wife?

01.

How has seeking your wife's approval shaped your behavior, and what has it cost you?
Reflect on times when you have altered your words, choices, or even personality in hopes of gaining her affirmation. What parts of your masculine strength have been lost in this process? How can you take them back?

02.

005. A MAN OF YOUR WORD, GOVERNED BY PRINCIPLE

03.

What is the difference between being a source of refuge for your wife and being someone she has to mother?
A wife needs security. She doesn't want to carry the weight of leading her husband. In what ways might you have unintentionally made her the leader in your relationship? What specific steps can you take to reestablish yourself as the man she can safely rely on?

04.

What does it mean to truly "take it back" as a man of Principle?
The chapter speaks about reclaiming authority over your actions, decisions, and leadership. What are some areas in your life where you have surrendered control? How can you take responsibility and step into your role as a leader in your home and marriage?

005. A MAN OF YOUR WORD, GOVERNED BY PRINCIPLE

05. **How can you balance listening to your wife's heart while also maintaining your own independent identity?**
God calls husbands to both love and lead. How can you honor your wife's emotions and wisdom without becoming dependent on her for your sense of self? What does this balance look like in daily interactions?

06. **How would your wife describe your leadership right now? How would she describe it if you became the Man of Principle God designed you to be?**
Think honestly about how she sees you today. If she could describe her ideal, strong, rooted husband, how different would that man be from who you are now? What's stopping you from becoming him?

DANIEL LIFE CHANGE

Daniel's life embodies the heart of Chapter 5, as he was a man of unshakable Principle, refusing to waver in his convictions no matter the pressure, threats, or consequences. He did not let external forces, fear, or even the risk of death dictate his actions—instead, he lived by a higher law, his allegiance to God.

His story challenges us to become Men of Principle who govern ourselves not by fleeting emotions, external approval, or cultural pressure, but by the truth and convictions we've chosen to live by.

Daniel refused to cave to external circumstances forced on him by the surrounding culture, seen initially in his refusal to eat according to the Babylonian customs.

And throughout his life, he's never seen looking for permission or approval, even when it meant that he would risk death in order to continue following his principle of worshipping the true God.

We also see him embodying a brilliant mix of submission to God, coupled with authority, influence, and honor. He commands respect from everyone around him, even the enemy king and his henchmen.

005. A MAN OF YOUR WORD, GOVERNED BY PRINCIPLE

DANIEL

For each section of scripture below, respond with the most jaw-dropping, earth-shattering truths that the Holy Spirit reveals to you.

What do you notice about Daniel's life, decisions, character, and confidence that you want for yourself?

Remember to ask the Holy Spirit to apply the Scripture uniquely to you, to take it from a distant historical truth, to his specific message to YOU. Ask him to plan this type of manhood into your spirit TODAY.

DANIEL 1:8-21

Points to consider: The virtue of disagreeability, Daniel's confidence in conflict, faith that God will honor your convictions

DANIEL 3:1-30

Points to consider: The courage of Daniel's three friends, their absolute faith that God "WILL" deliver them and give them victory, refusal to compromise

005. A MAN OF YOUR WORD, GOVERNED BY PRINCIPLE

DANIEL 6:1-28
Points to consider: Daniel's favor from both God and men in authority, his own authority even over lions, his steady demeanor and lack of panic

REFLECTION AND GROUP DISCUSSION
- Where in your life are you allowing culture, circumstances, or approval-seeking to dictate your principles instead of deciding them with God?

- Daniel didn't wait for permission to live by his convictions. Where have you hesitated to step into what you know is right because of fear of disapproval or rejection?

- What is the "king's food" in your life—the thing everyone around you accepts as normal, but you know is not for you?

- Are you willing to face consequences for your convictions? What compromises have you made in the past out of fear, and how can you correct them moving forward?

005. A MAN OF YOUR WORD, GOVERNED BY PRINCIPLE

MODEL PRAYER
LIVING AS A KING

Father, I come before You today, ready to step fully into the man You have created me to be. I am done living according to shifting emotions, seeking approval, and being tossed by circumstances. I want to be a Man of Principle—a man whose word is solid, whose actions are governed by truth, and whose life is ruled by Your wisdom, not by fear.

Jesus, You have called me not only to serve but also to reign with You. You have given me authority, not to dominate or control, but to govern my own life with integrity, courage, and unwavering conviction. Teach me what it means to rule well—to carry myself with honor, to speak truth even when it costs me, and to stand firm in my decisions with confidence, not insecurity.

I repent for the ways I have wavered, the times I have let others dictate my values, and the moments I have allowed fear to silence my voice. No longer will I be swayed by the moods, opinions, or expectations of those around me. No longer will I hand over my leadership to anyone but You.

Today, I take back my role as a man who leads with strength and love. I will live by the principles You have placed on my heart, not because I have to, but because that is who I am. I will be a husband, father, and leader who is steady, unshaken, and dependable—a safe refuge for those entrusted to me.

I declare that I am not a servant to fear, approval, or passivity. I am a son of God, a man of dominion, a king in Your Kingdom. I will walk in my authority with humility and power, just as Jesus did.

Thank You, Father, for trusting me with this life. I choose to govern it well, in full submission to You, and in full confidence of who You have made me to be.

In Jesus's name, amen.

0

MASTER YOUR ALLEGIANCE

006

6

MATT HALLOCK

MAN WARRIOR KING

CHAPTER SIX
YOU ARE ENDORSED

This chapter opens with a discussion of Aslan's interaction with the White Witch in C.S. Lewis's *The Lion, the Witch, and the Wardrobe*. Focusing on his flash of anger that surged when she quesitoned whether he would stay true to his word.

But there's another VERY important scene from the Prince Caspian movie, towards the end, when Lucy stands on her own on one side of the river, facing the bridge that connects to the opposite riverbank.

The fleeing enemy army is headed straight for the same bridge from the opposite side of the river.

She clearly presents an unimposing, non-threatening appearance to the enemies. And as the enemy leader looks around at his options--either backward into the pursuing armies of Narnia, or forward into Lucy, all alone--the choice is clear. Press onward to fight and push past Lucy.

But then, before the enemies have a chance to truly charge her, Aslan emerges, calmly and confidently walking up to her side.

The implication: he endorses her.

If she will be bold enough to stand and prevent the enemy from taking her territory, then HE will stand with her and meet her will with his power.

This is what he wants to do for you.

Where are there enemies advancing that you need to take your stand against?

What will you allow in your life? And what will you fight back against, to kick it out?

This has everything to do with being a Man of Principle, who uses the power of his will, his decision, to shape the entire atmosphere--the ecosystem--of his life.

You have to understand that when you speak and decide a thing, Heaven responds to your decision.

I know that's backwards from what you're used to. And I know that it may challenge some deep mindsets in you.

But that's okay. Scripture does indeed prove this out.

Take some time to read Matthew 16 and look closely at the words of Jesus about who will prevail against whom, about what happens when you bind and when you loose.

You'll see that YOU are the causative force, and heaven's actions are the response.

MASTERING OUR ALLEGIANCE

01. The book argues that our allegiance is often revealed not just in our actions but in our thoughts. If someone could read your mind for a full day, what would they conclude about where your allegiance truly lies? Would they see unwavering faith in God's promises, or would they see doubt, fear, and compromise, agreement with hell's thoughts instead?

02. The chapter makes a bold statement: "Your circumstances do not define God's will—His Word does." In what areas of your life have you allowed your experiences to dictate your theology instead of aligning your theology with God's Word?

006.   MASTER YOUR ALLEGIANCE

03. **In this chapter, I challenge you to "cut the head off" of negative thoughts that contradict God's truth. Think of one major area in your life where you feel stuck. What false narrative have you been telling yourself about this situation, and what is God's truth that needs to replace it?**

04. **Proverbs 18:21 says that "death and life are in the power of the tongue." If your words are constantly shaping your reality, what kind of world have you been building with your speech? How have your words unknowingly given power to either life or death in your circumstances?**

006. MASTER YOUR ALLEGIANCE

05. When things don't go the way we expect—whether in healing, finances, marriage, or personal growth—it's easy to assume that God is indifferent or unwilling. How can you shift your perspective from measuring God's will by your experiences to anchoring yourself in His promises, even when you don't see immediate results?

06. Is thinking "realistically" truly beneficial? Or is it limited? Is it a way of squashing faith and instead living only by what my senses perceive rather than by what God TELLS me? Jesus said, "According to your faith will it be done to you." How has your belief got you the results you currently have? How can you uplevel your belief?

CALEB LIFE CHANGE

Chapter 6 talks all about how our thoughts get shaped by our circumstances and how those circumstances make us feel.

The truth is, most people go through life being led around by whatever feelings are the most natural to arise within any given circumstance.

Not Caleb.

Caleb, and his buddy Joshua, trekked into the promised land and saw all the same cities, all the same giants, all the same dangers as the other ten faithless spies.

But instead of giving in to the doubt and fear, he doubled-down on bold, reckless, audacious faith. Faith in what God had previously promised.

"I'm giving you this land."

Then, when Caleb had to wait 40 years...he was just as fervent, committed, and confident as ever:

"Give me my hill country."

And he got it.

How will you be like Caleb...believing more extremely in God's promise than everyone around you?

006. MASTER YOUR ALLEGIANCE

CALEB

For each section of scripture below, respond with the most jaw-dropping, earth-shattering truths that the Holy Spirit reveals to you.

How does Caleb's grit, determination and dogged faith inspire you to believe--to really BELIEVE--God at his word?

Remember to ask the Holy Spirit to apply the Scripture uniquely to you, to take it from a distant historical truth, to his specific message to YOU. Ask him to plan this type of manhood into your spirit TODAY.

NUMBERS 13:25-33

Points to consider: Their enemies, the available blessings, the fear of the people, the focus on negativity

NUMBERS 14:1-10

Points to consider: The complaining of the people, Caleb's rebuke, fear as rebellion, trust in what God said, confidence in our ability to take the land

006. MASTER YOUR ALLEGIANCE

JOSHUA 14:6-15
Points to consider: Caleb's patience, his strength that was built through his faith, his commands to give him the land, his fearless eagerness to fight out the enemies

REFLECTION AND GROUP DISCUSSION
- Where are you still letting "giants" look bigger than what God already said you could have? What would it look like to see differently this week?

- Who around you needs to see your bold obedience so they can believe for their own? How could you believe publicly, not just pray privately?

- What area of your life, right now, needs to transform into looking like God's fulfilled promises instead of giants roaming and waiting to devour you? Have you given up in that area? How can you reignite your faith there?

- What does it look like to "move mountains" through your words, your prayers, and your faith? How can you eliminate doubt, even after waiting as long as Caleb did?

MODEL PRAYER
A DIFFERENT SPIRIT

Father, I refuse to see the world through fear's eyes anymore. I've spent too long agreeing with giants, and doubts, and all the tactics of hell. But You have said the land is mine.

You have said I am well able to take the promises. Teach me to see through Your eyes—to believe You more than I believe my memories, my failures, or the size of what stands in front of me.

I repent for every time I've given into defeat and complacency. Forgive me for walking with the majority when You wanted me to stand apart.

Today, I align myself with Caleb's spirit—a different spirit. One that clings to Your promise even when others complain. One that grows stronger and bolder with time.

I declare that the fire in me is hotter today than ever. I will take my mountain. I will not die in the wilderness of caution or regret.

Let me walk as a man fully convinced that You are faithful. I choose courage, conviction, and your promises.

This land belongs to You, and therefore, it belongs to me.

In Jesus's name, amen.

A MAN OF PRINCIPLE
PART TWO
CAPSTONE

MATT HALLOCK

MAN WARRIOR KING

A MAN OF PRINCIPLE
- PART TWO CAPSTONE -

MY RESUME, FULL OF VICTORIES AND REDEMPTION

One of the biggest threats to your ability to live as a Man of Principle is your past. Past sins. Past failures. Past mistakes. Past wounds. Past trauma. Past decisions. Past abandonment. All of it.

Go to church on Sunday and look around the sanctuary at the men sitting in their pews right along with you. I want you to know something.

Most guys at church do not feel like they are thriving. Most feel some sort of nagging ache somewhere inside their souls. And many times that ache is rooted in regret or guilt or some other form of self-accusation.

These thoughts and feelings tell them, "You'll never amount to much. You've wasted your chances, many times over. You'll always be limited by your past, your upbringing, your failures. The best you can do now is to thank God for the fact that he's blessed you with a family and a good job even though you don't deserve either."

I'm telling you, negative self-talk (which is really making agreements with negative "hell-talk") is deadly. And it will destroy your soul if you let it.

So in this exercise, you're going to create your own Kingdom Man's Resume.

The purpose is to begin to reframe your past so that it only fuels you toward winning and no longer can sink its fangs of regret and shame into your heart and mind.

It's going to take a few steps to get it done, so stick with the process.

A MAN OF PRINCIPLE
- PART TWO CAPSTONE -

MY RESUME, FULL OF VICTORIES AND REDEMPTION

STEP ONE:
Watch the bar fight scene from the movie, Secondhand Lions.

- Head to Youtube and search for "Respect your elders - a clip from the film Secondhand Lions"

- Alternatively, scan the QR code and it will take you right to that video:

- Take note of how Robert Duvall KNOWS who he is. He confidently runs through the history of his achievements and experiences in such a way that presents him clearly as a force to be reckoned with. A man who should not be crossed.

- Is this how you feel about yourself? If not, why not?

STEP TWO:
Read Genesis 16, Romans 4, and Hebrews 11:8-12,17-19

- Pay careful attention to the factual record of events, as they happened in Genesis. Notice the weakness, the sin, the failure of Abraham to truly and fully believe God.

- Then, notice the way in which God chooses to speak of him in Romans 4 and Hebrews 11. There's no mention of Abraham's doubt. In fact, it appears almost as if God is LYING about him! God says he didn't doubt at all!

A MAN OF PRINCIPLE
- PART TWO CAPSTONE -

MY RESUME, FULL OF VICTORIES AND REDEMPTION

STEP THREE:
Make this yours.

- Let the way God chose to honor Abraham in the New Testament really sink in for you. Let it speak to you of his forgiveness...but also more than that...his complete removal of your sin.

- Abraham isn't paying the price for his doubt! Instead, he's getting honored for his faltering and imperfect faith as though it was flawless.

- My goodness! That's incredible mercy! That's incredible generosity and favor! It's like God rewrote Abraham's past so that there was only good left!

- And this kind of redemption of your past is available to you too. But you have to accept it.

- **Follow these instructions for the following page:**
    - In Box 1, bullet point your life's victories and failures. These are actual things you've done...not qualities about who you are. List your victories first, in the top half. List your failures second in the bottom half.

    - Journal with the Lord. Ask him how he sees your failures, according to Abraham, as we talked about in the lesson.

    - In Box 2, write down the reframing of your failures. The redemption of them. Redeem your history right now with the Lord.
        - Instead of, for example, being addicted to alcohol, in box 2 you'll write that you're a man who's overcome alcohol.
        - Or instead of being cruel and harsh with your kids, in box 2 you'll write that you're a man who has faced anger and cruelty head on, and won.

    - In box 4, write out your Man Resume, listing in powerful succinct points what you've done. What you've achieved. What you've overcome. Remember Secondhand Lions.
    -

A MAN OF PRINCIPLE
- PART TWO CAPSTONE -

MY RESUME, FULL OF VICTORIES AND REDEMPTION

BOX 1:
PAST WINS AND LOSSES

BOX 2:
REFRAMING THE LOSSES

A MAN OF PRINCIPLE
- PART TWO CAPSTONE -

MY RESUME, FULL OF VICTORIES AND REDEMPTION

BOX 3:
MY KINGDOM MAN'S RESUME

A MAN OF PRINCIPLE
- PART TWO CAPSTONE -

The objective of this exercise is to articulate and seal your personal code as a man of the Kingdom.

Fill in these statements as thoroughly as possible, with everything you can think of. If you need more space, do this in a journal or in a computer file of some kind.

Make sure you keep this accessible so you can keep referring to it.

One of the men I've coached did something that I absolutely loved. He invited his wife and kids out to the back yard to have a mock burial ceremony as he said goodbye to the old man that he used to be. It was powerful.

When you are done with this creed, feel free to do something similar, to bury, as a prophetic act, an object or handwritten note that symbolizes the old way of doing life.

I RENOUNCE... (OLD PATTERNS, FEARS, IDOLS)

A MAN OF PRINCIPLE
- PART TWO CAPSTONE -

I EMBRACE... (KINGDOM PRINCIPLES YOU LIVE BY)

I STAND FOR... (CORE TRUTHS)

A MAN OF PRINCIPLE
- PART TWO CAPSTONE -

I FIGHT FOR... (PEOPLE AND/OR MISSION YOU PROTECT)

"Jesus, You are my King. My allegiance is Yours alone. Let these guiding principles shape my every thought, choice, and word until my life fully reflects Your Kingdom."

SIGNED: _____

03. PART THREE

PART THREE
A MAN ON MISSION

MATT HALLOCK · DNA TACTICAL GUIDE · MAN WARRIOR KING

07

RECLAIMING YOUR FIRE

007

MATT HALLOCK

MAN WARRIOR KING

CHAPTER SEVEN
YOUR MISSION NEEDS YOU

At the start of Chapter 7, I share the story of the first healing miracle I ever prayed for.

This moment marked a turning point, a momentous ship-burning.

There was no going back.

I want to invite you to that same moment.

But there's a problem: our modern theology.

We unfortunately have a dearth of faith in today's church world. We THINK we have it, but we don't.

We have any number of reasons why NOT to believe God, and when someone comes along who does believe him, we question their heart, their sanity, and even their salvation.

But stepping into his mission for your life REQUIRES that you do it **His** way...not the way of the theologians, or the seminaries, or even the pastors.

So the first hurdle that you need to jump is your intellectual objections to the power of the Kingdom...if you have any.

The second objection to overcome is the more personal one: "There's no way God would ever use ME that way."

Truthfully, if we have intellectually accepted the present-day working of the Holy Spirit in signs and wonders, we often get stuck in the prison of self-doubt and self-deprecation.

"I'm not good enough to do amazing things."

"I'm too timid to even try. God wouldn't show up for ME."

Take a moment to journal with the Holy Spirit. What is standing in the way of you living on Mission and advancing the Kingdom with power and miracles?

DESIGNED FOR MISSION

01. What is it that keeps you from waking up each day on mission? Is it a struggle for survival? Is it disappointment? Is it self-doubt? Is it a fixation on a certain problem that has convinced you that you don't have any fuel for your mission? How can you rise above and embrace Mission on a daily basis?

02. Do you see yourself as a man who multiplies in his life? Or do you see yourself merely as a use of space? Take a moment and think about multiplication...What would your life look like if you multiplied your money, your joy, your health, passion in your marriage, his presence and his Kingdom? What old religious thinking has to die in order for you to fully embrace multiplication as your God-given mandate?

007.   RECLAIMING YOUR FIRE

HELD BACK BY BAD THINKING

01. Do you feel apologetic for merely existing? Are you afraid to assert yourself because of how it might inconvenience the world around you? What would life feel like if suddenly you weren't allowed to apologize for 30 days? You just...were. Where did this "over-apologizing" come from in your life?

02. How can you flip the flow of energy in your daily life? From "what's going to happen TO me" to "How can I happen to the world?" Take a moment to think about and write down 3 ways that you can give value to the people around you...today. Your wife. Your kids. Your co-workers or customers. Your church. Your neighbors.

MARRIAGE: MISSION VS MANIPULATION

01. When you think about your wife, are you most readily filled with a sense of swelling joy and enthusiasm? Or a sense of pain and dread? In other words, are you more consumed with how to give her value, or with how to GET value FROM her? How can you begin to shift in to offering value instead of NEEDING it?

02. Where have your acts of love become subtle negotiation tactics? Be honest: when you do something kind or romantic, what outcome are you secretly hoping for? If your wife never responded the way you wanted, would your love still be strong and alive — or would your "service" dry up?

MARRIAGE: MISSION VS MANIPULATION

01. When you think about your wife, are you most readily filled with a sense of swelling joy and enthusiasm? Or a sense of pain and dread? In other words, are you more consumed with how to give her value, or with how to GET value FROM her? How can you begin to shift in to offering value instead of NEEDING it?

02. Where have your acts of love become subtle negotiation tactics? Be honest: when you do something kind or romantic, what outcome are you secretly hoping for? If your wife never responded the way you wanted, would your love still be strong and alive — or would your "service" dry up?

007. RECLAIMING YOUR FIRE

03. If indeed she does feel like your acts of love are simply ploys in order to get what you want back from her...does this give you any insight into why she might feel unloved, unseen, and unsafe? What if she's not just cold and broken, but she's been starved of REAL love? What will you do differently now?

04. How have you made your wife your mission instead of your companion in Mission? Where have you placed her as the object of your purpose rather than a partner in your calling? What has that done to her energy, trust, and attraction toward you? Has it made her feel more like your mother than your sexual lover?

007. RECLAIMING YOUR FIRE

05. What would leading from mission look like today? Picture your day through the eyes of a man on assignment, not a man seeking comfort. How would you show up differently in your posture, your communication, your decisions? Write one concrete act of mission-driven leadership you'll take in your marriage within the next 24 hours.

06. If your wife could describe your energy in one sentence, what would she say? Not your intentions — your energy. Would she say it's peaceful, confident, secure... or grasping, anxious, and expectant? What needs to die in you so that her spirit can breathe again?

007. RECLAIMING YOUR FIRE

START SOMEWHERE

01. What's the "garden" God has already given you to work and keep? Every man dreams about global impact, but too many also neglect the small plot right in front of them. Where is God saying, "Start here"? What people, responsibilities, or areas of life need your leadership and full presence right now?

02. What excuses are hiding under your theology? Many men disguise their fear in spiritual language — "I'm just waiting on the Lord." In reality, they're stalling. Where have you disguised unbelief as patience or humility? What small, concrete act of obedience could break that waiting cycle this week?

007. RECLAIMING YOUR FIRE

03. **What distracts you most from your mission? God wanted for Adam to not elevate Eve above his calling. What beautiful, good thing in your life has quietly become an idol — something that steals your focus from God's assignment and calling on your life?**

04. **When was the last time you "set your face like flint"? Think about the last time you pushed through fear, fatigue, or opposition and stayed on task until breakthrough came. What did that cost you — and what did it produce in you? How can you rekindle that resolve in this season? What area of your life needs you once again to "set your face like flint" toward your mission?**

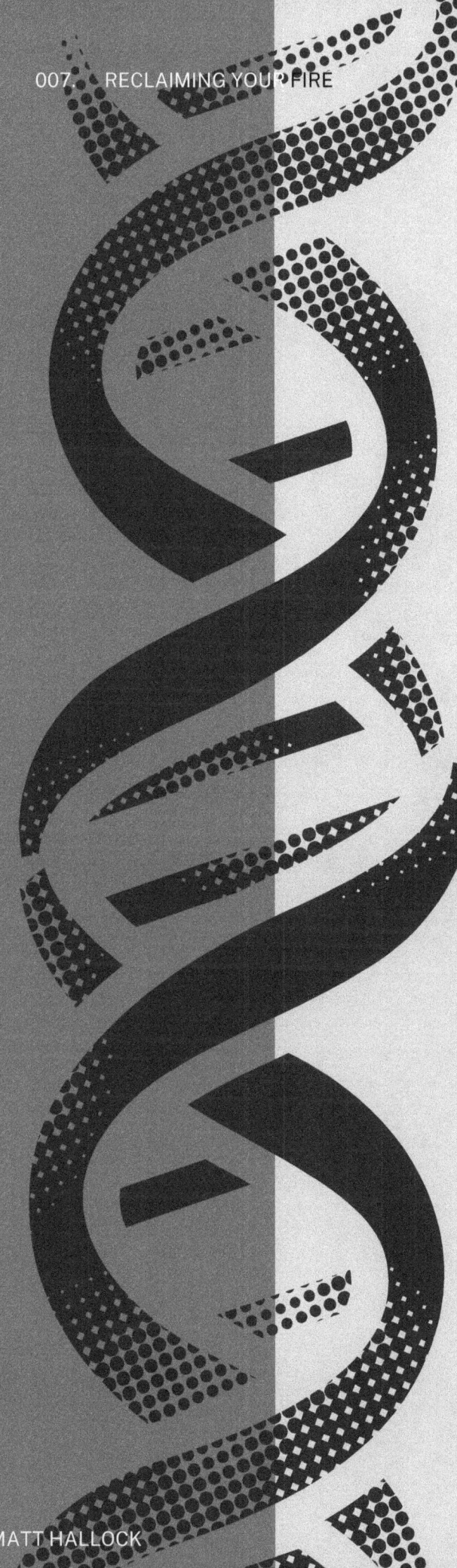

JESUS LIFE CHANGE

In Chapter 7, we learned how you and I are hardwired for mission, not for self-gratifying comfort and ease.

We learned that we are meant to assertively go forward and give value to the world, rather than apologize for our very existence, and for the inconvenience it must be causing the people around us.

We also saw how important it was for Adam (though he failed) to keep his mission front and center, and to not let his wife become top priority.

In my opinion, Jesus models all of these quite masterfully.

He was never focused on how the world might either harm or help him, he knew that HE was the store of life-force and so his energy was always flowing out...to give life.

He was exactly who he was, even at the cost of the approval of men, at the cost of being liked, at the cost of losing followers even!

And he models for us perfectly how a bridegroom can love his bride with everything he's got, while at the same time never compromising his identity or mission for the sake of her approval.

007.   RECLAIMING YOUR FIRE

JESUS

For each section of scripture below, respond with the most jaw-dropping, earth-shattering truths that the Holy Spirit reveals to you.

How does Jesus embody a man who is completely self-governed, totally unshaken by the opinion of others around him?

Remember to ask the Holy Spirit to apply the Scripture uniquely to you, to take it from a distant historical truth, to his specific message to YOU. Ask him to plan this type of manhood into your spirit TODAY.

JOHN 6:1-15

Points to consider: The focus on feeding others rather than on "what am I going to get?", his refusal to be moved by the doubt of others, his confidence in his mission and authority, compassion

JOHN 6:16-24

Points to consider: No limit to what he (and you) can do, walking on top of challenges rather than sinking in them, redefining normal, your mission makes others uncomfortable...oh well

007. RECLAIMING YOUR FIRE

JOHN 6:25-71

Points to consider: Offering sustenance and life to others, being a resource rather than a drain, knowing who you are...your identity, being ready to offend others, the virtue of disagreeability

REFLECTION AND GROUP DISCUSSION

- In the feeding of the five thousand, a boy's small offering became the miracle. Where in your life have you been waiting for God to act — when He's actually waiting for you to bring your loaves and fish?

- Jesus walked into the storm, not away from it, and peace followed His presence. How can you carry that same calm authority into the storms around your marriage, work, or health?

- Where is God calling you to speak or live boldly in truth, to speak your conviction, even if it costs you approval or comfort?

- What assignment in your life have you delayed or abandoned because of discouragement — and what would it look like to finish it with the same endurance as Jesus?

006.   MASTER YOUR ALLEGIANCE

MODEL PRAYER
BECOMING A LIFE-BRINGER

Father, thank you that I am a man who carries your life, and I bring that life into my world every day. Your life in me is powerful, it heals broken people, and it dissolves chains that keep them stuck.

This mission and identity that you've willingly handed to me is too precious to let it flounder anymore.

I declare to you today, that I will always, every single day, wake up to give value, to impart life, to be a blessing, to overflow.

I am a man of wealth, with more than enough to give to others. I am the solution to problems. I am the cure to brokenness. I am the wisdom in difficulty.

None of this is my own, but it flows through me from you, Father, the source of all good gifts.

I am done seeing myself as bankrupt and ineffective.

I am instead surging and bursting with the power of heaven.

I will accordingly live out my mission with confidence, passion, and grit. No matter who agrees, disagrees, or abandons me in the process.

O

HOW TO BE LEGENDARY

008

8

MATT HALLOCK

MAN WARRIOR KING

CHAPTER EIGHT
HOW LEGENDS ARE MADE

You, my friend, are a legend. You are one of the heroes of Hebrews 11, those guys who've been immortalized in the words of God himself because of their fierce faith, their unparalleled boldness, and their commitment to their Mission.

You might think, "No Matt, you don't understand. I'm not the same as them."

But you are.

And your first step to finally believing that is to stop declaring that you're NOT.

Write a brief declaration thanking God that you too are a legend.

Have you ever given much thought to your life mission in the past?

Have you considered that every single thing you do in your day can either be on Mission or not?

Or have you compartmentalized your life so that some of your activities are just the mundane necessary evils?

Take a moment to ask the Holy Spirit to change your mindset so that you truly see **every** activity as an opportunity to advance your Mission.

Ask him to teach you that their is no neutral ground in our life.

Everything you do can be wrapped in heaven's presence...if you choose to make it so.

WELCOME TO LEGENDARY

01. If someone watched your last month of choices, what creed, or Mission, would they say is driving you right now? Is it the one God wrote into your DNA, or one built on survival, self-preservation, hustle and grind, worry, self-pity, etc.?

02. You are the connecting point between heaven and earth — a living intersection of the supernatural and the practical. When was the last time someone encountered heaven because of your presence? How could you live going forward so that heaven encounters happen more consistently because of YOU?

008.   HOW TO BE LEGENDARY

03. When you read the Bible, do you approach it as a record of what God did—or as a mirror showing you what He wants to do through you? What would change in your day to day if you expected your life to look like the book of Acts, not merely cheap shadow of what once was?

04. You say you're connected to God's power source—but where in your life is that power actually visible? Where have you quietly agreed with the lie that "God doesn't do that kind of thing anymore"? How has that unbelief shaped the limits of what you attempt, pray for, or risk?

008.   HOW TO BE LEGENDARY

05. Isaiah says, "You will hear a voice behind you." How practiced are you at quieting the noise of logic, advice, and fear long enough to hear that voice? Where are you still living by pros-and-cons lists instead of by the Holy Spirit's whisper? What's one practical way you could build space in your week for this kind of listening?

06. When was the last time you obeyed God in a way that looked irresponsible to others—but proved faithful later? If you can't remember, what might that reveal about the level of risk you're currently willing to take?

NOAH AND ABRAHAM

01. What is God asking you to build that looks and feels foolish? Is he asking you to step out in faith when it makes no sense, when there's no rain in sight, when there's clearly no need for an ark? Where do you need to repent of doing life according to "the system" instead of His word?

02. Abraham failed and doubted, yet God still called him righteous. What mistake or failure have you used as an excuse to stop moving forward in obedience? What if God still calls you righteous? What if your mission is not lost, not shattered? What if you're not overlooked? How can you get back on mission under the banner of righteousness, not failure?

008.   HOW TO BE LEGENDARY

YOU CAN BE A MIGHTY MAN

01. Whose voice told you you're not enough? When did you first start believing you're not "that kind of man"? The fighter. The leader. The risk taker. The one God actually uses. Be honest — whose voice planted that lie, and how long have you let it run your life?

02. David didn't rebuild his kingdom alone — he gathered broken men around him. Who in your life right now is in distress, in debt, or bitter in soul — and might be waiting for you to call them into something higher?

008.   HOW TO BE LEGENDARY

03. **What part of your life have you treated as separate from the Kingdom? Is it your job? Your marriage? Your finances? Your sex life? What would it look like to make that part of your daily mission field?**

04. **Are you focused primarily on surviving? Or learning how to reign with Jesus in this life? How do you show up at your job, in your home, with your family? Is it as a man grinding to get by, or as a son of God sent to bring order, excellence, and Kingdom power into those places?**

008. HOW TO BE LEGENDARY

Who needs you to be their mighty man today? Whose life will be radically altered when you finally believe that YOU are the right man for the job? Is it your wife? Your son or daughter? Your coworker? The guy limping down the street? What if YOU are the one who brings hope, life, and victory to these people around you?

05.

008. HOW TO BE LEGENDARY

FEAR IS NO EXCUSE

01. God is telling you today that you are enough, that you don't have to be perfect in order to be used by him, valued and honored by him, one of his most valuable players. Do you believe him? If so, what are you going to do about it? If you don't believe him…why not?

02. Is it possible that the miracles listed in Mark 16 are actually possible for YOU to do? Have you seen them happen in your life before? What was that like? What did it inject into your soul to see heaven touch earth? If you haven't seen them, why not? Have you tried? What's getting in the way?

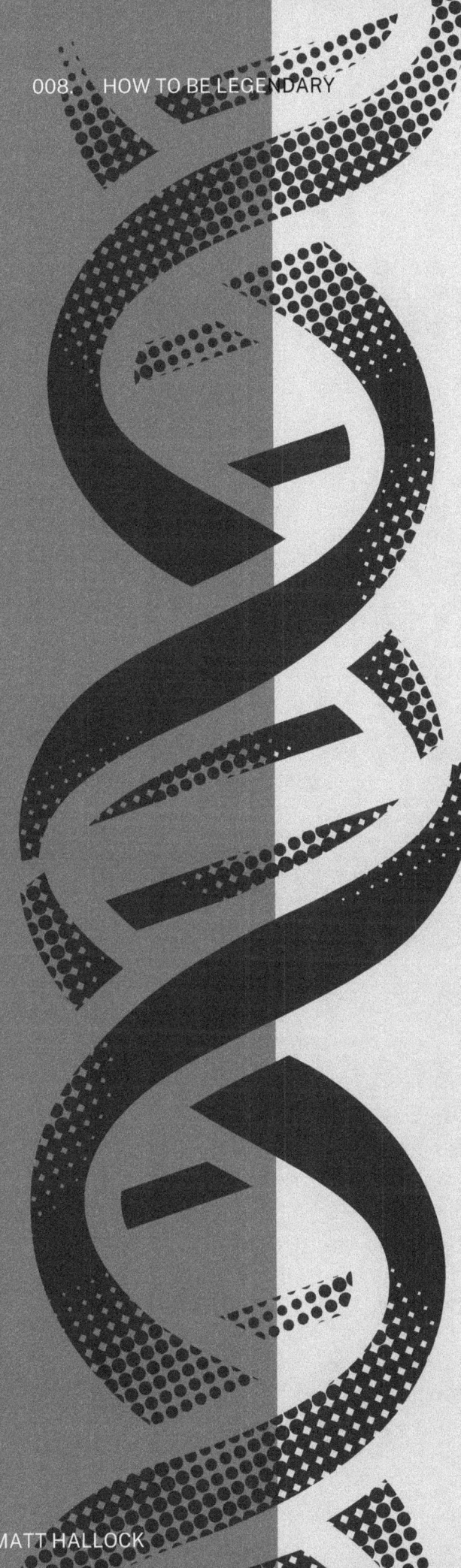

PETER LIFE CHANGE

The problem with this prospect of becoming legendary is that we feel so strongly that we just...aren't.

We fail.

We have stains on our past.

We have stains on our **present.**

We can't possibly imagine how to rise above the muck of the status quo to enter into a legendary Kingdom life, full of miracles and power.

Peter is a fantastic comfort, my friend.

Far from perfect, he too was drafted into the starting lineup, if you will.

I want you to look at his life, again, not as cool stories that God included in the book he wrote...but as an example for what your life can look like too.

Peter is nothing special. He's you. He's me. He's as many of us as will believe God when He tells us that we're good. We're okay. We can let go of our shame and run forward with full abandon into the MIssion of God in our life.

Let's never swim another day in our life. Let's walk on the water too.

008. HOW TO BE LEGENDARY

PETER

For each section of scripture below, respond with the most jaw-dropping, earth-shattering truths that the Holy Spirit reveals to you.

How does Peter get ushered into a surprising life of the supernatural, of miracles, of power like he never knew before?

Remember to ask the Holy Spirit to apply the Scripture uniquely to you, to take it from a distant historical truth, to his specific message to YOU. Ask him to plan this type of manhood into your spirit TODAY.

MATTHEW 14:22-33
Points to consider: Jesus' words enabling Peter to walk on water, the gumption and assertiveness of Peter, his initiative, the removing of limits in Peter's life

LUKE 5:1-11
Points to consider: Peter's old life of fruitless toil, the prosperity that Jesus brought upon him, Peter yeilding his boat/business, financial provision, favor, joy

008. HOW TO BE LEGENDARY

JOHN 21:15-19

Points to consider: Restoration, total forgiveness, getting back on Mission, forgetting about the past, freedom from shame and guilt

REFLECTION AND GROUP DISCUSSION

- When have you experienced Jesus pulling you up after you sank — and what did that teach you about His view of you?

- Jesus told Peter to launch out again after he'd failed at fishing all night long. What "empty nets" in your life make you hesitate to try again? Is it possible that Jesus is telling you, "Now is the time, let's do this again"?

- Why do you think Jesus asked Peter three times if he loved Him? What in you still needs that kind of restoration? How would it feel to know that you are fully restored?

- How does Jesus reinstating Peter change your opinion of your own failure? Do you think he even sees it? Or is it removed from you, nailed to the cross?

MODEL PRAYER
THE MAKING OF A LEGEND

Father, I step into the fire willingly. You've called me to be more than ordinary, and I refuse to shrink back into safety anymore. I was made to rule, to subdue, to bring Heaven down into this dirt and dust.

So, train me, God. Forge me like You forged David's mighty men—out of brokenness, fear, and failure, into power, strength, and reckless obedience.

I break agreement with smallness, with fear, with the excuses that have kept me stuck. You didn't ask for perfection—you asked for courage.

So, even if while trembling, I choose to move.

I choose to believe that You see something legendary in me.

Help me to live for something worth dying for. Fill me with Your Spirit of power, love, and a sound mind, and send me out as Your man on mission—one who doesn't just talk about the Kingdom, but brings it.

I declare today that you have made me dangerous. Legendary.

In Jesus' name, amen.

A MAN ON MISSION
PART THREE
CAPSTONE

MATT HALLOCK

MAN WARRIOR KING

A MAN ON MISSION
- PART THREE CAPSTONE -

ADVANCING THE KINGDOM WITH POWER

In Part 3 of *The DNA of a Man*, I articulate two different types, or levels of Mission in your life: 1) Your grand, overarching mission to advance the Kingdom in every way you can, and 2) your smaller, more specific-to-you mission, or missions, that has a practical container, pursuit, job, or goal/dream.

This exercise will focus on the first one. And particularly, on opening up to the task of advancing the Kingdom using **every** means that God has made available to you, namely...power.

Our modern church culture has long been held hostage under the sway of the lies from hell that signs, wonders, miracles, displays of power have all been done away with in our day, and in our location.

Without this real, present, active, now working of the Holy Spirit, our advancing the Kingdom assignment becomes one of mere human skills of persuasion, administration, programming, and intellectual study.

Too many men have been fed this lie, and have consequently been fed an automatic mindset of:
- What I believe isn't all that believable. Part of it isn't even true anymore.
- God himself didn't even see fit to put me in an era where I would get to seem him do miracles. Makes me feel somewhat left out if I'm honest.
- So rather than run forward, full steam ahead...I have to tame myself. Put a lid on it. Settle for a less-than version of Kingdom living.

Do you see the danger here?

It's time to break out of this self-imposed prison and come alive in the power of the Holy Spirit once more.

Let's do this!

A MAN ON MISSION
- PART THREE CAPSTONE -

ADVANCING THE KINGDOM WITH POWER

STEP ONE:

Read the Scriptures commonly used to promote the idea that the gifts and communications of the Holy Spirit are not applicable in our era. Read them as though you were a little child listening to your Father's instructions. Would that be the most obvious conclusion you'd form from these verses? Why or why not?

Please keep a journal close by while you read...and write down what the Lord shows you

- Ephesians 2:18-22
- 1 Corinthians 13:8-12
- Revelation 22:18-19
- Hebrews 1:1-2, 2:3-4
- Jude 3

STEP TWO:

Read the following passages, again as a child would listen to his Father. Not as an adult would dissect, and inject an agenda, and reason about. A child simply hears and believes. Simple.

Keep a journal and write down what God shows you about miracles, his power, whether it's for you today or not.

- Acts 1:8, Acts 2
- Mark 16
- Matthew 10:1
- James 5:13-18
- 1 Corinthians 12:1-11
- 1 Corinthians 14
- 1 Corinthians 4:20

A MAN ON MISSION
- PART THREE CAPSTONE -

ADVANCING THE KINGDOM WITH POWER

STEP THREE:

Just start.

We often come up with all kinds of busy work to do that is a mere procrastination of just doing the ACTUAL WORK.

Not so here.

Your task is to step out into DOING two of the various kinds of miracles we see in the New Testament. These are the two I have the most experience with, and two that really excite me.

Healing and prophecy.

I know that these can raise ALL KINDS of questions, and perhaps I'll need to write a future book on how to step into a life of miracles. There's benefit to more teaching that will build your faith and give you more detailed mechanics as to HOW...

But I can tell you, while most Christians are waiting on God to go ahead and just do the miracles finally...he's actually waiting on YOU to start.

Healing:

Choose one person this week to proactively pray for healing. Do not do this on your own at home from a distance for the person. Go to their location, call them, and pray directly in their presence.

Maybe it's someone you know, or maybe it's a stranger whom you happen to meet while going about your normal day. Although, to be honest, I think you'll have a higher chance of success if it's a stranger (not enough room to explain why here).

A MAN ON MISSION
- PART THREE CAPSTONE -
ADVANCING THE KINGDOM WITH POWER

Healing (continued):

Here are the steps:

- Ask the person if you could pray for them really quickly, because you know they're hurting/suffering and you also know that Jesus doesn't want them to suffer. (It must be from love and compassion, not "because I want you to become a Christian")

- To yourself, tell Jesus that you KNOW he wants everyone healed. All sickness and physical pain were handled by his blood.

- Pray short and sweet. Do not ask God to do the healing. You yourself must command it to happen. Talk right to the body part and tell everything good to be healed. Tell everything bad to leave, get out, dissolve, etc. Tell all pain to leave. Tell range of motion to return. COMMAND THE SITUATION.

- When finished, ask the person to check to see if it feels different. I know this is the scary part, but it will DRASTICALLY increase your success rate if you don't skip this.

- If nothing changed, pray a second time. Third time. And more. As many as you have courage for, and THEY have patience for!

- If still no healing, tell them you'll check back in a few days and pray again, if you know them. If not, thank them for their time and tell them how much you and Jesus love them.

- If they do feel it getting healed, then I think you'll be able to handle it from there :)

A MAN ON MISSION
- PART THREE CAPSTONE -

ADVANCING THE KINGDOM WITH POWER

Again, you may feel like you need a LOT more training on this stuff.

That's understandable.

If you're brand new to this whole kind of thing, then you might want some teaching that will build your faith and really get you pumped for this kind of lifestyle.

But it's not REQUIRED in order for you to just **start**.

It's a matter of, "Does Jesus want me to do this?"

Yes or no.

If yes, then, "Am I going to obey him?"

Yes or no.

It's that simple.

A MAN ON MISSION
- PART THREE CAPSTONE -

YOUR LIFE'S MISSION STATEMENT

Write down three areas of your life that once burned with passion, conviction, and faith — but have since cooled off. Maybe you grew tired, weary, discouraged, or something similar. Be brutally honest. Where did you stop believing God could move through you?

Now, for each of those 3 areas, name the exact mindset, fear, or disappointment that extinguished that flame. ("I got burned out." "I thought I missed my chance." "I stopped expecting God to show up.")

How are you going to resurrect your fight in these three areas? How are you going to reclaim your mindset from the grip of those limiting thoughts and lies?

A MAN ON MISSION
- PART THREE CAPSTONE -

YOUR LIFE'S MISSION STATEMENT

Now, let that realization for where you let your zeal and faith fade...let it inform how you process this next piece.

REALM OF YOUR LIFE	WHAT IS GOD NUDGING YOU TO BUILD, FIGHT FOR, OR MULTIPLY?
MARRIAGE	
FATHERHOOD	
WORK/BUSINESS	
MINISTRY/COMMUNITY	
PERSONAL GROWTH	
HEALTH	
MONEY/WEALTH	

Now ask yourself/ask the Holy Spirit: "What would heaven look like if it fully broke into this area through me?"

Are there any additional lies or mindsets that are keeping you stuck in these areas?

A MAN ON MISSION
- PART THREE CAPSTONE -
YOUR LIFE'S MISSION STATEMENT

Next, I want you to craft a three part personal mission statement. You're going to do your work in this workbook, but I want you to type and formalize a more pretty copy that you can keep with you, post in your office, etc.

1. Who you are (Identity: who God says you are).
2. What you do (Principle: what you stand for and will not compromise).
3. Why you do it (Mission: the heaven-to-earth outcome of your life).

If you need, there is an example at the end of this exercise

Sentence 1: Who you are (Identity: Who God says you are, and who you've decided to be)

Go back to your Part 1 capstone assignment and look at your chosen Identity scriptures, your personal Identity statements that you came up with for yourself.

See if you can find common themes, powerful words that jump out at you, compelling phrases from those that you can use to distill all of that into a single sentence.

Use this space to jot things down and brainstorm.

Sentence 1:

A MAN ON MISSION
- PART THREE CAPSTONE -
YOUR LIFE'S MISSION STATEMENT

Sentence 2: What you do (Principle: what you stand for and will not compromise)

Go back to your Part 2 capstone assignment and look over your different responses there, especially under the Renounce, Embrace, Stand for, and Fight for sections.

See if you can find common themes, powerful words that jump out at you, compelling phrases from those that you can use to distill all of that into a single sentence.

Use this space to jot things down and brainstorm.

Sentence 2:

A MAN ON MISSION
- PART THREE CAPSTONE -
YOUR LIFE'S MISSION STATEMENT

Sentence 3: Why you do it (Mission: The heaven-to-earth outcome of your life)

Think through how you want to make heaven known through your life. How do you plan to give your life in service of the King. What drives you when you wake up every morning?

What makes your day more than another day of the rat race? Of survival? Of just getting by?

Look at your Life Realms from this Part 3 capstone, and see what God is asking you to do? What is the common theme that he's speaking over your life in each separate area and all at once?

Use this space to jot things down and brainstorm.

Sentence 3:

A MAN ON MISSION
- PART THREE CAPSTONE -

YOUR LIFE'S MISSION STATEMENT

EXAMPLE:

I recommend that you allow yourself to make each sentence a little on the longer side. Think through how you want to husband, how you want to minister, how you want to work, how you want to father, how you want to think, and incorporate all of these into your statements.

In fact, you may need to start out by having 2-3 sentences within each part...and you can continue to refine and condense from there.

There is truly no one right answer, but do attempt to cut out extra wording and get it to a really concise and potent mission statement by the time you're finished.

Sentence 1: Identity

I am a son and warrior of the living God, a fiercely loyal and attractively confident husband, and a vigilant father.

Sentence 2: Principle

I bring order, healing, and strength to everything under my influence through my commitment to love, honor, and faith as I seek to protect my wife and children, help and serve those around me, and go boldly in the direction God leads me, regardless of anyone's opinion.

Sentence 3: Mission

My life exists to make the presence of God tangible in every environment I enter, whether through miracles, surprising love and generosity, or boldly speaking truth (whether it's popular or not), and I do so each day, regardless of how I feel, who is watching, or what I'm needing.

A MAN ON MISSION
- PART THREE CAPSTONE -

YOUR LIFE'S MISSION STATEMENT

BRINGING IT ALL TOGETHER

Sentence 1: Identity

Sentence 2: Principle

Sentence 3: Mission